A WELL-MANNERED STORM

For Alex,
A pleasure to meet you
at the Sechelt Festival!

[signature]

Caitlin Press

A WELL-MANNERED STORM

The Glenn Gould Poems

KATE BRAID

Caitlin Press Inc.
8100 Alderwood Road
Halfmoon Bay, BC, V0N 1Y1
www.caitlin-press.com

All photos courtesy of SONY BMG, photographer Don Hunstein
Author photo John Steeves
Text and cover design by the house

Printed in Canada

Caitlin Press acknowledges financial support from the Government of Canada
through the Book Publishing Industry Development Program and the Canada
Council for the Arts, and from the Province of British Columbia through the
British Columbia Arts Council and the Book Publisher's Tax Credit.

**Canada Council
for the Arts**

**Conseil des Arts
du Canada**

BRITISH COLUMBIA
ARTS COUNCIL

Library and Archives Canada Cataloguing in Publication

Braid, Kate, 1947-
    A well-mannered storm : the Glenn Gould poems / Kate Braid.

ISBN 978-1-894759-28-1

    1. Gould, Glenn, 1932-1982--Poetry. I. Title.

PS8553.R2585W44 2008   C811'.54   C2008-904826-1

This book is for John

Contents

Contents (cont'd):

Contents (cont'd):

Dear Mr. Gould,

What do I know about music? But today I heard Partita No. 6 in
E minor (BWV 830 is what the cover said) and my throat closed,
hearing you talk like that. Those top notes, so light, ached like rain
over drowned fields, such heaviness underneath. What do you think
of when you play? Why so sad? I hope you don't mind me writing to
you. It's the sadness that gets me.

Sincerely,

k.

Dear Glenn Gould,

I can't stop listening to Partita No. 6. I tell my friend, "You've got
to listen to this," me with tears in my eyes and when he listens, his
eyes light up like a kid who's just been given a chocolate Easter egg.

"Epiphany!" he says. His fingers twitch, he sways his head—heck,
his whole body—he's having a good time on Partita No. 6 but me,
Glenn, I'm almost lost in the sadness and only the light of your
confidence leads me through. You know something and I want to
know it too.

In grief,

k.

Dear Glenn,

Me again. How do you stand it, music that wears such a heavy over-coat and paces, that likes a good downpour and strides forward with a solid step, unafraid of the dark? Some people call it romantic. Ha! Like heartbreak is romantic until it's your own.

So how do you do it, head up, hands wide? Or is it precisely in the hands, that welcome? Refuge as something you can get your hands on. A short romance, glorious one night stand affirming, "I was here, all here. See these hands?" Go for it, you Romeo.

Feeling better,

k.

Spring Walk

Toronto in the '50s. Think fog. Think
white dough.

I walk these streets, *staccato*
of my heels, clap clap

on concrete and snow,
one precise step after another

to the icy counterpoint
of a single crow.

This is Bach walking to somewhere beautiful.
Walk itself. Fog lifts. I am fed.

Partita by Johan Sebastian Bach

The left hand begins it,

right hand rises, trembling

to conduct.

If one wants to concentrate, one must bend,

lean

forward

over the heart

pouring, *largo*.

For this they laugh at me.

This is the erotic of music

unspeakable

white touch, naked

under dazzle,

the moment of letting go

lifting.

Where would you like the feather of sound

to touch you? Lighter,

longer?

At the end, I promise,

you will be breathless

and crying.

Why Bach?

Shelter, of course, solid as Chartres,
certainty the sky will not fall as you rest
under the pillars of such harmony,
stained glass and light, a blessing.

Here are elegant black-mounted marble steps, entry way.
Choose any room you want: kitchen warm with wainscotting—
a solid chair rail to catch you if you fall—and there,
a quiet corner for thought, buttressed by books.

Who, fastidious, would not want to live here?
Even the messy and careless find shelter.
Especially the careless. Enter here.
Amid such order, see how the languid toss
of a scarf, scarlet against the warm brown of polished wood,
cool slate, see how the outline of silk on stone, startles.
Suddenly you've never seen such silk. Close your eyes. Rest.
If you wish, you can hide inside these walls,
sustained. Here, you are safe.

Dear Glenn,

It was years ago I first heard you play, when a friend played me your second version of the Goldberg Variations, by Bach. I never liked Bach. Too complicated, too boring. Doesn't go anywhere, I told my friend, but he insisted so I listened. That was all. I'd never heard of Glenn Gould before that.

Years later—last year—I was driving on September 25, your birthday, and on CBC Radio Margaret Pacsu said that after you played her your radio documentary, The Idea of North, she cried, and you, who didn't like to be touched, wiped her tears with your handkerchief.

I was on my way to be with my mum who'd just been diagnosed with cancer. Something about the crying, the handkerchief, the tenderness of your gesture made me listen more closely to the music that came after—Bach, I think—made me wonder who you are.

> *Sincerely,*
>
> *k.*

Lesson for a Beginner

You can't just listen to the notes, no,
you must listen for the spaces between.

Think of a picket fence, glimpse of a yard,
peekaboo pattern of a woman in her lawn chair,
the hem of her blue and white cotton dress,
green garden, red hair, a hand. Languid.

See how the pickets are essential
so if you tore the fence down
the yard would not be the same yard, the woman
not the same woman. Without the puzzle, the frame,
it all becomes common and bare.

Or think of a hill at sunset, the jagged truth of maples
against skyline. Lazily you take in the hook of hill, *larghissimo*
but there, look harder. Bach is that line where sky and trees meet,
black against blue like a tattoo on you.
Some fear it. Some never see it,
a whole new landscape. How transformed,
irresistible the view.

Those Voices and Chalk

In my too-formal shirt and tie,
they put me up against the wall, boy
who hums to himself, who conducts
invisible orchestras. Weird one.

After school, sons throw stones and jeers,
timpani of fists and spit.
Mothers barely hold them back.

Teachers send home question marks.
I am ordered, Go play! and they don't mean music.
My only desire is for harmony
and I am assigned the drone of History.

I hide in thickets of Haydn, Mozart, the fog
of Beethoven—can't catch me there.
All morning my body (drum skin tight)
waits for the school bell, refuge
of tone rows in the tapping of teacher's fingers,
children's voices and chalk.

I think of every cruel story I dare not tell,
every childish lie, every word I've ever regretted,
every fearsome wish, and imagine all these
made beautiful and right with music.
I imagine being forgiven.

What have I done wrong, Mother?

Recess

My back presses against the wire mesh fence
that separates me, schoolyard
from my own backyard.
Exile.

I hear Mother
through the kitchen window, calling.
The bars between us.
A single gull flies over, grey.

Becoming

I was six when my parents took me
to my first piano concert—
Josef Hofmann—and in the car,
coming home, half asleep
I heard orchestral sounds
and I was Hofmann.
That's when I knew
I could become another
and later, fishing,
a living perch on my line,
this thing—twisting
extension of my breath
iridescence of sea and me—
for the first time I knew it
from the fish's point of view.

When the neighbour raised his hand to kill it
I screamed and stamped my feet,
almost tipped the boat
until he let it go.
I would die if he did not stop.
I knew what we shared, that fish and I,
more than breath
the way his body leaped,
grey rainbow of scales,
the brightness of his eye.

Transformer, that's what I am. It's easy.
I slip my edges like shedding
a too-large coat (thin skin)
for another, larger
and am lighter, the ghost of me free
to become Brahms, Webern, Bach.
Especially Bach.
Where do you care to go? I can take you there.

My Plans for the School Year by Glenn Gould, Grade 13

Found poem

I am at somewhat of a disadvantage in writing on this subject, for my adventures in the halls of learning are curtailed at the close of the fourth period each morning. The remainder of my day is spent in the pursuit of music, with the exclusion of an hour or so in the evening which I rather grudgingly bequeath to Macbeth, the Treaty of Ghent, and the subjunctive mood.

It must not be assumed, however, that I have a complete disregard for higher education. On the contrary, I find it is stimulating, enlightening, refreshing and capable of tremendous influence on otherwise stagnant minds. (For this well-defined phrase I am indebted to the preface of a Manitoba school textbook authorized and published in 1911, entitled, "Crop, Cricket and Tariff Control.")

My course of study includes only three Upper School subjects, French, English and History. I consider this a most happy choice, for, in French, one reads Rousseau and sides with the revolutionaries; in English, one reads of Wellington and sides with the reactionaries; while in History, one writes critical analysis of the Milan Decree and the Orders-in-Council and shows how much better everything would have been if only some enlightened fifth-former had been present at the Congress of Vienna.

My plans for this season include a number of solo recitals and appearances with the Hamilton and Toronto Symphony Orchestras. Although very little of this is relevant to the title, I think it will be sufficient to show why I have not a moment to spend on extracurricular activities at school. My plans for the school year, therefore, are non-existent.

I am going to attempt, however, to have a fairly inclusive notion of the curriculum by next June. And now, I think that I shall assume my most scholarly and penetrating visage, and devote this next hour, not too grudgingly, to "Macbeth."

Shadow

don't come too close
or you'll see

shadows. mother
half-hidden
watches
handcuffed

there are no handcuffs! only
a trick of the light

but can you see
her hands extended

begging,
a command?

she always wanted her son
sole child, to be famous

I would do it for her.

Dear Glenn,

My mum's surgery went well but yes, it's been a rough year. After her diagnosis I went deaf in one ear. It happened overnight. A cold, my doctor said, and prescribed antibiotics, more antibiotics and finally, a hearing test. Permanent inner ear damage, the specialist said, and turned away. What does that mean? I've made an appointment with another doctor.

Then for some reason I can't remember, I played your recording of the Goldbergs. I turned my right ear, the good one, to the speaker and when the piece was over I was curled in front of that speaker, crying. What did I hear? What did you say, what did Bach, that I had to listen again, over and over. Isn't it a miracle, that when I lost half my hearing, Bach changed too?

(I dare to say) Your friend,
k.

The Preludes by J.S. Bach

i.

Prelude in C Minor

Outside is dark. Inside, the warmth of a slow fire and himself humming,
how he'd walked to church that morning,
the bright flower of his youngest daughter's hand,
the extraordinary blue of the sky, a breeze
that lifted the curl on Anna Magdalena's cheek
as she walked beside him.
His, hers, the child's steps, a counterpoint clear as glass
on the fine gravel of their walk to blessedness.
And when she turned to look at him
her eyes that same blue of sky, he did not startle,
only his heart fluttered a little before he went on.
Later, he would write about it.

ii.

Prelude in D Major

Now water dances, a ripple, a wave, a shoulder shove,
the pattern of centuries of silt.

He makes a small, passing mark no larger than a trout's egg.
Still

it is a living thing, a mark someone else
will be grateful for. He doesn't know

where the ripples might lead,
what shape they might take.

The Secret

You can reach out for the ideal by imagining it, of course.
—Glenn Gould

What is a piano? Workhorse
grazing on music. Box
with a lyre inside, its pedals the reins
with which to make it work harder.

Instead of thumping away at a heartless wooden chest,
instead of letting my fingers tag after its hollow shape,

I imagine.

This is where I go.

As if someone has passed before me
through tall wet grass
and I can see the way. Clearly
light shines off it. I follow.

Dear Glenn,

When I told my father about my ear, he whispered into the right one, the clear one, a lullaby he used to sing when I was a kid and couldn't sleep.

When I asked my mother what she'd do if I went deaf in both ears, she said, "I'd cry. Then I'd learn sign language."

In luck, like you, with my parents,

k.

Ice Man

The image of me out there—Ice Man—
it's only image. I don't want to show
how it all comes from the blood, from inside, you know?
I only tell you this now because I'm drunk on sound.
Tomorrow I will deny it.
Blood? What blood? I am Bach.

Dear Glenn,

Bach didn't change all at once. I loved the Goldbergs but others—The Art of the Fugue, The Well-Tempered Clavier—were too hard to understand. Until I read your essays that said there is no narrative line in Bach. "If one could express it in cinematic terms," you said, "Bach was a director who thought in terms of cuts rather than dissolves."

So you see, I was right—Bach goes nowhere! But the next time I listened to The Art of the Fugue I listened harder and this time I heard it, ecstasy in each moment. I'd been looking too far ahead and all along he was here, all of him, right under my ears. Or should I say, ear? I cried then too—a real crybaby lately, aren't I!

I don't know why I'm telling you this, Glenn, so personal. I just wanted to let you know you've been a comfort—all that beauty in my good ear.

With thanks,

k.

Epiphany with Vacuum and Fugue

At the age of ten I wasn't much attracted
to multi-voiced things. But as I practiced a Mozart fugue,
the housekeeper switched on the vacuum cleaner
to stop me, so I couldn't hear the notes

and I was sucked into a storm of sound
with only an imagined Mozart and my fingers
on the coolness of keys.

I met the fugue that day, threw myself forward,
fingers slipping over the silk and stone of notes
like a blind man led to shore who sees
the sound of surf, cry of gulls,
rough scrape and rhyme
(the breath) of granite pebbles,
shock of salt. Cold

subject and answer,
a conversation, surge and swell
of counterpoint.

Guerrero

Our hand is part of our mind.
—Alberto Guerrero

One does not play the piano with one's fingers,
one plays the piano with one's mind.
—Glenn Gould

It was Mr. Guerrero who, shall I say "helped"? me.

It was my gift, after all, and truthfully
I held it to me, I now confess, perhaps
a little too tightly.

But Guerrero was there. And Mother.
They taught my fingers to be light. The Goldbergs.

Me? I tried not to look at the battlefield,
all those black and white bodies.

It was Mother got me humming
Guerrero said I was unteachable. You see?

When one meets the music one yields
hands, body, everything.

Ahh! There was no teacher.
Inevitability taught me.

Performance

I take simple precautions with my health
(coat, hat, muffler, two pairs of gloves,
the weather doesn't matter)
and they market me as some kind of freak,
vaudevillian.
How eccentric is it to keep my fingers warm,
sit bent to the keys so I can hear the music coming?

I play with my fingers flat and light,
feed the notes the quick sweetness they call for.
Savour.

I do apologize for singing. But
some pianos cannot do it alone and I must help
however I can, music a pearl that waits to form
around the ten dark seeds of my fingers.
What could matter beside that?

Did I Sing?

I hummed, I drummed
my feet, conducted
myself and anyone else
who'd pay attention, or not
whole carols, anthems, hymns
my body
a pulse and thrum
vibrating, pendulum
a rhythmic
throb and flutter
in a roll and pitch
see-sawing, a diving board its
upward oscillation a palpitation
the room a seismic
lurching all those pitching
microphones a-flutter
and I ask,
(an aside to the engineer
beside the tape recorder,
open-mouthed)

Did I sing?

In the Doctor's Waiting Room

He is late. Again. I sit, trembling,
urgent in my need for pills.
An impatience of others waits with me,
all of us, our anxious breaths baited every time
he returns to call another:

Next! Next! Next!

I have surveyed each of them, judged
what ails them, scanned every magazine,
played the last scene of *Capriccio* in my mind, twice,
considered leaving but hold instead, sit
staring out the open window

Next! Next!

at maple trees. There seem more of them today,
branches random in a crisp breeze. Light lands
on the top branch, lower ones
shadowed, a forest of emerald and pearl,
rhythm of *allegro, molto allegro*, a chime
of dip and praise dip and praise   dip.
Behind them, a string of hazy blues
and the counterpoint of oak moving
as music, whole and healing.

Next!

Birds' Bach

Yesterday I played Bach's Partita No. 4 in D Major
and a bird sang outside the cottage window.
I went on: Partita No. 5 then 6
the Variations and Italian Concerto
and there it was, a robin I think, as if in tune
and more, the Gigue from Overture in the French Style
Chromatic Fantasy in D Minor the Praeludium in C
Major a finch a sparrow and another, something
I couldn't place, a whole symphony, a Bachanalia of birds,
all of us winging it and me just warbling along.

Hi Glenn,

They warned me; in the same way two eyes give depth for sight, two ears give direction for sound. I have no sense now of where sound comes from—not voices, not a bird's call, not a siren.

One night after it happened I was running the bath and a bee flew in, loudly bumping into walls. I looked to my right, always further right until I was turning in tight circles, lost in my own bathroom. I never did find that bee. I opened the window and he found his own way out.

Wishing you stereo hearing forever.

                    Your friend,
                    k.

Song

One note
rises like grass
a melody of green
oratorio, majestic
cricket.

A Certain Order

It is imposed

        kindly

    because we all know
                chaos

inevitable
      grief.

Bach says
        just for the moment

let go

   as if all is

        perfect

        right
as is.

Isn't that just

         music
  music

    to your ears?

The Goldberg Variations (1955)

Aria
is the empty platter
white, on which is served
colour, sound sweet
as dusky dark figs,
tart as limes, round as apples,
each flavour
its own course.

The Variations
An entire meal and the conversation around it,
the click and clip of the tongue, dentals
hard white and smooth
tongue rolling round
the curl of an unshaved cheek.
Imagine it—
the licorice and peppermint of piano keys,
sweet and savory of Bach.

Variation 15 in particular
If there is loss you can act
as if in control, stepping carefully,
matter of fact between the lines of your life.
If your feet feel heavy, you tell yourself
it's all in the head, the heart
and carry on, eyes fixed.
If a tear falls you say, "Fog!"
Something has fallen into you.

Count your steps. You are growing a garden
of heartaches. Do it well, tend it.
When rain falls, open your arms.

Aria da Capo

Coming home, sated now—
some say there should be gladness
but you say no. There is still grey,
the fullness of rain falling,
fruit and flavour for some other day.
What is left will be an emptiness
not like before.
This will be the emptiness of a photograph,
emptiness of a room once lived in, a room loved.
After, you will vibrate and tremble with that memory,
that emptiness, opening,

after.

Glenn,

There's nothing to one side of my body. A heavy fog, impenetrable, in my left ear. The left side of my body is dark but that ear is a curled conch shell, silver, with a stopper.

It's only one ear, though sometimes there's also a crackle, fullness in the other. I try not to think of it, whatever "it" is, spreading. Try not to think of not being able to talk to friends, hear birds, your music.

I can't hear anything over a running tap. Now I understand why spies turn on the water—microphones have just one ear, too. It makes me nervous to see people—even on TV—sitting to someone's left. How can they hear? I avoid restaurants, the clang of cutlery, voices, the hum of fans.

Isn't it funny—all those overlapping voices are only exhausting to me while I struggle to hear with one ear. But they're music to you, inspire you to contrapuntal radio.

> Your friend in wonder,
>
> k.

A Brighter Rain

I lie on warm earth staring up through a maple at bolts of sky,
grapes scattered like green bees over the picnic table.

Just how long can I play with the long black chords
of "Onward Christian Soldiers" scourging me from behind?

I rest, envious of seagulls wheeling in the wide grey sky.
All that solitaire, all that open against heaven.

I am knocked about, a rag doll bleached by Bach. What more
would you have me do? Even surrender is too much.

You want to know what I hear? I hear snow, everything that melts.
I hear deep rock, flowing. I go there often, step through.

I am not here. Only my hands. I follow them. Sing
with medieval choirs. Step there, and back. Always a traveller.

One hundred words for snow? One hundred words for *legato*, the slow pace
of river running, melt, bees a-hum, the silk of grass, rain under a sheer storm.

People say I am a great pianist and this is true
but I am modest before the music.

On the fascination of cold keys: like playing on ice.
My tongue stuck to glory.
Ratushinskaya says grey is the colour of hope. It is also
the metallic glitter of necessity. On another day, simply rain.

Bach is good table manners, crunchy granola and that little bit of oats
stuck between your teeth that your tongue can't forget.

Bach is rain shadow, avalanche, hush, a caution, whodunit
and your favourite teacher reading love poems. Bach is my shepherd.

Did you ever have to walk too slowly? A grey moss, dull rain, old man's beard.
Not knowing how deep it goes, how long it's been there.

No Other Sound

God help me if I have to endure one more concert performance one more hacking gagging snorting caterwaul of cough, one more walk along the gang plank to the haven of piano, all rattled and broken by the pandemonium, sputter and gob, atrocity of audience.

If only they'd be quiet! Who let them bring in their chewing gum candy bar bloody lunch wrapped in waxed paper and the Sports section anyway? Here's impossible: reaching for ecstasy while someone wheezes in your ear, tears wrappers off his Juicyfruit his cough drop—slowly—and balls up the scraps in excruciating crackle.

Save me.

You know that infamous symphony, The Water Torture, by Cacophony? They think if they do it slowly they're doing me a favour. What do they think they're here for? Entertainment? It's hard work, losing yourself. Leaves my body hanging cold, icicle swinging in the breeze of their bedlam. After each performance I am lost. There are no candy wrappers there, no sound but the still paradise of Bach. Silence.

The Art of the Fugue by J.S. Bach

You can listen to it as a complication. Or?
Nothing else. Unless

simplicity itself. In layers.
Think lace. Think steel.

The decomposition
of silence and sound.

Blank page, lines and spaces
imminent. Think snow

as it covers your mouth, buries you
beautifully

a pointillist painting
of zeros and ones

that ravishes you and doesn't care,
leaves you bleeding, begging

and as you fall, caresses your forehead,
hums a hopeless lullaby.

On Tempo

Always trust in the difficult.
—Rainer Maria Rilke
Letters to a Young Poet

By slowing them down, I open them
(the Siegfried Idyll, Brahms D minor)
while the critics have at me.
Funereal, they say, and *Hallucination. Betrayal*, even.
But listen. If you walk more slowly, do you not see more?

The difficult sustains me.
When I am parched and dry
here is my refreshment—a single stone
tossed off-centre in the pond,
carpet of sun laid to the edge of water,
glister of light.

I wait on such sweetness, embrace
the slow pace, warm trickle of blood
as heart opens. And again.
A sudden sunbright streak of emerald,
the taste of green, salt of stone, *lentissimo*.

Though the balance be more difficult
how alive now the underbrush, that maple,
the peculiar chatter of squirrel,
heartache of a single fingerprint on glass.

Fugue No. 10 by J.S. Bach

Each note drops
dark water
in a slow
slide
into the next

cool

if you are the water
you'll know where
to go

slipping

become
one bead
breathing
a breeze
ruffling your calm

now

sound, song
a single tear
and light
your closed eyelids

see

by sound
one note is all
one other

its cool
black
bead.

Loneliness

Isolation is the indispensable component
of human happiness.
—Glenn Gould

The critics, the world, even some of my friends think it mysterious
I am so much alone. They think I must be lonely. Don't they know?
Isolation is the indispensable component of human happiness.

Some days I bundle up, get in the car, turn the heat and radio on high (this is the best)
and drive around Toronto, sweating. It's a story rarely told, for
the critics, the world, even some of my friends would think it mysterious.

When I was young my friends were Nick the dog, Mozart the budgie and four fish:
Bach, Beethoven, Haydn and Chopin.
Isolation is the indispensable component of human happiness,

not a wife, not a close friend, no. Instead I take the splendour of music, peerless
companion that accompanies me to that place where order lies, home,
though the critics, the world, even some of my friends, think it mysterious.

Each hammer stroke on string, each fading note, precious,
can be called at my desire again. How much better even than the telephone.
Isolation is the indispensable component of human happiness.

Music is my wife, its shimmer of constancy, wondrous.
What lover could keep such harmony and still forever come when called?
The critics, the world, even some of my friends, think it mysterious
but *isolation is the indispensable component of human happiness.*

Borders

My body arches and grows fur.
My ears, my hackles rise.
That's not an innocent hum in my throat.
I am a guard at my own borders.
Too many have crossed them uninvited.

What no one knows is that my fangs
were drawn, my nails clipped, long ago.
I cannot bite. I take the blow,
a wound, inside with me.
You cannot come here no matter who you are,
here, inside the fortress of fugue and partitia where
notes, like hands, heal me.

Glenn,

When I was a kid I loved church—that moment of passage, step from the chatter and dark of vestibule into the high brightness of sanctuary. Outside to inside, the caul of the ordinary, dropped.

In church, nothing was casual. Every step slowed, charged with a larger meaning. It was peace and order in a vast container, the ritual of bending and rising, amen. You know what this is. Today as you played Bach I heard it again, that sacred space. You call it ecstasy.

Thank you,

k.

The Last Puritan

I am the last Puritan. It's a name that sticks
to me, a man who makes no aesthetic judgements
of others, only moral ones.

Bach operated within the same severe code:
kindness, honesty, the straight and narrow course,
his love (I dare to say love) focussed
in a single zealous channel,
isolation if it must be. No god but this—
a narrow gorge between whose stern walls
fresh floods of music rush at will, freed,
focussed by the certainty of a close course, thin lines
of a musical score, white page.

All of it for the zest of cold spray, fierce foam
that turns wheels, floods a page
with the raw rush of music. Heat.

No Metaphor

Bach is an explosion of simultaneous ideas,
an *appassionato* of pattern. Nothing romantic

unless you believe in wonder. Notice
how this makes you want to sing.

F Minor

if I were a key I'd be F minor,
small grey stone skipping over water

F with its formal tone,
pleasure in the game

light
with the heaviness of rock

a *pizzicato* of Fs.
F is for fire, for *forza*, no fear.

here's what I know for sure:
grace. calling. a high note to end on. flight.

Call Me Doctor

A briefcase full of pills: Aldomet for blood pressure,
Nembutal for sleep, tetracycline for the constant colds,

Phenylbutazone and Allopurinal, Librax and Indocin,
Fiorinal and Valium for everything else.

Crude goalposts, they help me
stagger from one encounter to the next.

"Up" for the concerts (dread)
"down" for sleep.

One pill keeps the food down
another cures the ache in my gut, my shoulders,

hands.
When I am afraid, I take a pill

see another doctor. They don't need to know
about each other, about me

hanging from a prescriptive thread
only needing a little help

with this fragile web that bears me
(the gift) to the piano.

The Art of the Fugue by J.S. Bach

When I'm seated at the keyboard
     with Bach, I play as many parts as I can
and him the rest.
     I mean, hum the rest.

When I'm seated at the keyboard with Bach,
     my lips tingle
as if the music, not satisfied with my hands,
     wants my mouth also, palette and tongue.

Next thing you know I'm slippery with it,
     sweating Bach, dripping
fugues from every pore.
     Nothing, no limit,

every vein and artery
     lungs breath teeth and muscle
sinews all twitch in time
     a rising flood every cell a song

a sizzle a wiggle a polka
     a hula a waltz and
stillness
     impossible!

Glenny Jumping Bean here,
     ladies and gentlemen,
jiggling jelly on the spot!
     You think he's going to

let you loose let go but no,
        only a momentary slowing
largo largo lentissimo
        but it's not a relief no, because it

hard clasps you again
        to its hot heart and ready or not
you must dance
        yes yes
you must dance

and I
        must sing.

Burlesca

What has three legs, never walks, but transports you,
has no arms but embraces hundreds at a time?
What single key opens eighty-eight different doors,
is black and white but blinds you with its colour?
What silent visitor sits in your living room and sings?

Gould's Bach

People say we're *relentless, difficult, obscure.*
People say *quirky, unyielding, obsessed.*
Sometimes they say *eccentric, bombastic* and even
he fights against reason. Sometimes they say
genius.
Then, *he's nuts.*

I say, *architect.* I say *texture:*
brilliant, clear.
I say *honed to a fine intelligence,*
sword. I say *grief*
and *ecstasy.*

Shucking Genius

Celebrity lashes me like a whip.
I am slave to it. What I desire
is only the music—haven there.

I forbid them to clap, arrange silence and dark
and they're angry, clap anyway.
It's only their ears I want. Their hearts.

Instead it's *Ooh!* and *Ahh!*
He wears gloves! He hums along!
Why are they really here?

Genius! they say and suck me dry.
I wouldn't mind if they only fed off the honey
my hands can bring. If they wept.

Instead, I am bound and tied by their adoring,
sappy eyes—their own genius, abandoned.

Recording

In the recording studio, microphone
is my hammer.

Auditory architecture.

Ears, be my eyes. Give me a clear view
of this body, structure, precisely singing.

Why Webern: Concerto for Nine Instruments

One might imagine disintegration. Chaos, at least.
Bright city streets, sirens, too many trucks, people.
Webern is Small-Town-Meets-Big-City, the lights
too-bright crimson, cadmium, lime,
eighteenth century closing in on the twenty-first.

If not big city, try country circus. Here lumber the elephants
(sing to them, strangely light); there tigers
slipping through the undergrowth of people's legs,
pussy cats really, purring like cellos.
Here come fire eaters, horns aflame
and the sad clown of the clarinet.
There goes a prance of plucked strings and all along
the piano (did I say pain?) as ring master, host of the whole event
come to see it all runs smoothly.

Piano: eighty-eight stuttering strings along which
beads slip, fall like popcorn, promiscuous in the heat of my hand.

Did I say, order? Impeccable.
When my life is scrambled, in pieces, this is where I go.
To the solace of wonder—feral—every time.

The Idea of North

Found poem from Glenn Gould's
CBC sound documentary, *The Idea of North*

How does one reach an idea?

You go there over difficult terrain, trying the whole time
to talk to others so you can't spend too much time
up against your own sad self.

You arrive on a snowy cold day and there's no one there to meet you.
With no sense of direction, which direction is north?
What is most important? And who do you say hello to?

The north is re-creation, the chance to be alone, to be quiet.

"Emptiness" means getting lost in a style of your own.
"Frontier" means how you cope,
how you get along with yourself. How retreat.

If you're smart, you'll lose yourself behind a mask,
hermit by choice, focussing inward.

I met an old Swede, a gold seeker, who spread his gold out for me
and said, Take some. I said, I can't take your gold!
and he said, It's not the gold. It's the finding of the gold.

We pull north through monotony, together.
Are we? Bound together?
The alcohol is a symptom, a sort of protest.

North is an island; there's no escape, cooped up
in those wide-open spaces. All that freedom
with nothing to block your view, only
the fear of getting lost. All that space for terror.
No landmarks we recognize. No maps.

Community is a matter of life and death.
Pathetically, you sing along with the missionaries, the gossip.
You'll never know if you've chosen their company
for the peace it offers, or instead of madness.

It's this matter of life and death that diminishes you,
as if everything must have a form.

As if everything must have a form, we measure,
hang on to our own paper-thin dream.

What do you do when your patience runs out?

It's a love affair, this idea of north.
You can't talk about it until you're out of it.

I didn't miss women, I missed food: lettuce,
fresh vegetables.

In this country we complain, look for Utopia (no, not Toronto).
We have a built-in sense of direction that has nothing to do
with north, or any direction that is physical;
an inner gyrocompass that gives a sense of the possible,
points to a direction
where we don't recognize the land marks.

If the north were just like the rest of Canada
why would anybody go there?

William James said being "against" something
is what keeps us together.

We go north to the land of the possible.
We go north for the struggle, for the cleanness of coming up
against all that nature. The north is our moral equivalent of war.

Hi Glenn,

We were in New Mexico and passed by a Catholic shrine. I don't call myself Christian but I'm desperate—took a handful of "holy" dirt and pressed my left ear to the small plastic bag as if it loved me. But it didn't. Or not enough.

Odd though. The arthritis pain I've had in my hand—the one that took the dirt—is gone. A small miracle I wasn't looking for.

Your friend in trying anything,

k.

These Hands

If I pull off these woolen mitts of mine
or shake your hand, who knows what harm may follow;
my fingers, knuckles, wrists—the lot—confined,
compressed or chilled, doomed to be impossible and slow.
Disaster of the fiercest kind if these,
these slender bridges of flesh and bone, these paths
for me to Bach, Beethoven, Bruckner, Strauss
and all the rest should suddenly collapse.

It's all a piece. The clothes, the hands, the quiet,
my need to live alone, by night. I do
not weed or dig. No crushing tools. I've quit
all cooking, seek out greasy spoons to go
where no one knows me, wants to be my fan,
where no one knows me, wants to crush my hands.

Dear Glenn,

When you started going to doctors for your shoulder and the numbness in your fingers when you played, did people roll their eyes? Did they tell you it was hopeless?

I hate that people give up so easily, hate what's happening to me, how stupid it makes me feel. Pardon? I keep saying over and over. I want this to end.

Did you ever play that game: if you had to lose one sense, which would it be? From here, they all look so precious.

Why should I chart this for you? People say something good will come of it, some other sense will grow stronger but I feel only more sorrow, more loss, my left ear only good to hang an earring on.

I'm sinking, both ears full of water. Going under.

k.

Sleepless

Crossing the chasm of night on this raft
was once a fearsome pushing off
from the shores of day
from the work-ridden hours
into silence

eleven o'clock

twelve o'clock

two

sometimes the journey was timeless
through fogs of sleep. Other days

three o'clock

four

and waves of worry,
lists of to-do, people's faces,
the reefs of Call me! Call me! Endless
chores, obeisance, sometimes
it was enough to hold on through the dark
to the other side, to dawn,
the temporary safety of that shore

until the next night.
So tonight I shall stay on watch

awake, alert, the light
above the piano, soft silence of a city,
even the telephone
at rest, beautiful in black.
Now midnight shifts
from storm to port,
the peace of darkness and solitude.
I shall stay here. Hidden. At last.

Why Schoenberg

Someone asks how I could love Schoenberg.
Love? Do you love the mountain that lures you
up its brilliant slope, then tries to trip you?
Do you love the mustard plaster that burns
but cures the aching in your chest,
the rigid plaster cast that makes you whole?

Schoenberg was storm, the bolt of lightning
that tore open my boy's mind, hypnotist
who lured me into mountains, taught me
the boldness of ice, to ski
from one black tone to another.

Twelve-tone music is a synonym for noise; look it up.
He taught me it isn't all order. Or the order
isn't always what you think, not
skipping children holding hands in a polite line
but the unexpected leap for the rope's centre.

Order can be black and white, plain as polka dots,
or a clean cone of turbulence.
Here is the back side of order, danger climbed to its highest peak,
the view that takes your breath away.

The Three-Cornered World

I love a rocket thrill. I want the fastest car, the biggest sound board.
People call me reckless but really, it's so measured of me
to just sit here and play—Wagner or Webern—
all of it happening right before your eyes
even if my fingers do occasionally blur.

Did I tell you about the three-cornered world?
It's the one that's left when you take common sense away
from the practical and the everyday. It's the danger
of tearing one corner off the map of your life,
then turning the key to drive. Accelerating.

Northern Bach

*...haunting in its emptiness and bleakness
and starkly magnificent beauty.*
—Glenn Gould
speaking of the Canadian north

Snow and ice, especially ice.
The music gleams with it, blisters, blinds.
Sunlight off each struck note plays
in the key of icicle. Bach in a blizzard.
Each note an icy seed, footprint
in a field of white.

I deliver a northern Bach, exploring solo
in a whited-out world.
What matters? This step. The next.
Small dance along a path
that glistens with the heat of touch.
Black and white. Etched ice.

I'm alone on this trip. No rope securely anchored
to another explorer, front or back. No map.
Only one dark, overcoated shoulder, collar pulled high,
my gloves, cap, scarf already moving away, leaving a trail
of dark notes, single black flakes in a swirl of white,
a starkly magnificent score of ice

and faintly, the thin hum of a coated figure,
that sound, that thread that ties us all irrevocably together,
B-flat and A and C and B-natural...
echoes of a well-mannered storm.

Dreaming While on a Canadian Pacific Railway Trip Across the Prairies

It is minus ten degrees outside in the Prairie chuffing air.
Is this Winnipeg? Regina?
There is a small distance outside my window, a crystal of blue
cattle, not people, a whole herd of them, chuffing
(that word again) in the hard blue, dark blue night.

There's singing in them, small mountains
of peace. A mooing happiness.
When the chain, the nuts and bolts of the ordinary
are removed, a small song emerges. Name it: fugue. Name it: prayer
of blue fire, blue gentian, blue lord
who wanders, awe-struck beside a still river.
Who wanders? Who sings? A hallelujah of chuffing, ahh.

There is no formula for what goes on in these fields,
beside this river. Or it all depends on how you look.
It always depends on how you look.
Sun rising. The divine order, lightly golden now, the particulars
of time and space and sound. There's math in that relationship—
one tiny bee of sound after another.

This slow shedding of darkness, opening of a round black eye,
    utterly ancient.
The numbers are always here, the trickery-joinery of them,
smooth as a bellow. Now let be the zip of coming and going.
Joining. That's what I miss. The slow chuff
of joining note to note. The beauty of the numbers, frozen gold.

The Golden Number

> *True musical delight...consists only in apt numbers.*
> —John Milton

> *Music is the pleasure the human soul experiences from counting without being aware that it is counting.*
> —Gottfried Leibniz

> *When thinking as a mathematician, human bodies, emotions, and interpersonal relationships take on less and less importance, whereas the universe as an expression of number relationships takes on more and more. There are ecstatic moments.*
> —William Hamilton

Bach's math, extraordinary. Tight texts of sound in the book
of pleasure. He said, *The math doesn't matter. Only,*
how does it sound?
      But if mystery has a name, it is number,
or where's the delight? Number and proportion: everything
from this. Start with One, first point, mirror above the keyboard

in which I recognize myself. From the beginning my heartbeat
played counterpoint to my mother's as I lay curled in her belly.
Unity times itself is always unity
      'til it runs to the tension of Two.
Dual as discord but also twin-ness. Black and white keys
—there are only two. A line from there to here.

But if Two is the door then Three is the threshold to harmony.
Three phases to the moon, three layers to this small heart.
Three to reconcile opposites: Karl Marx knew it.
         First the point, then the line and now—finally—
the surface upon which I play. Then Four and structure, fair
and square. I go (God help me) to four corners of the earth

via eighty-eight keys to the kingdom. The slow cracks of soil
and Hebrew letters for Jehovah, all Fours.
There is no effort in numbers; fluid, the chart they draw.
         If mystery has a practice, it is number.
These fingers, Five—beautifully. Four elements
infused with life itself.

Puzzle: how do you plant ten flowers in five rows and still have
four flowers in each row? Think of a star shining over
the fertility of Five. Think of the symmetry of leaves,
         small hands open to the sun,
rising and falling precisely
in pattern.

Six is the wholeness of the honeybee's hive. Two times six,
an even dozen. Twelve constellations of the ancient sky, twelve
labours of Hercules. And so to the magic of Seven, virgin
         number indivisible:
seven days to the week, clean animals admitted to the Ark
by sevens (only the unclean in twos), seven years

for a field to lie fallow. And now behold
the sevenfold mathematics of music, how Seven loves Six,
or its double, beauty of the twelve-part

celestial canon visible
on the keyboard. Play with it:
Three times four equals twelve, Three plus four equals seven.

The seven colours of the rainbow are music made light.
Twelve-note chromatic scale (white keys), seven-note diatonic
(the black), all the shades of musical colour—*chroma*—between.
Do is for *Dominus*, Lord, Re is for *Regina Coeli*,
Queen of the Heavens, our small world below brimming
with divine chords.

We are a book sealed with seven seals, one of them my own
blood pressure, another, the mean temperature in Canada
on any given day. Here are all of us, balancing
precarious   precious   in the middle
we hope of all that number: 146 over 114, 154 over 116,
high of 11, low of minus 3.

The man on TV says "Chilly tomorrow," and means it.
There is a mathematical solution to everything. For example,
did you know everything beautiful is 60 per cent
of everything else? The Golden Mean
shapes my face (scalp to brow to throat), my arm, its golden
division at the wrist, length of each finger joint. I count,

catch numbers like fish in the fullness of their stream.
Like stairs, I mount them, counting. Some call it rhythm, some call it
line. I call it tide rising pull myself along a lineage as sure as knots.
If mystery has a face, it is number,
number as boat, as float, as a raft to rush me away
on torrents of order holding a tight

rein, taking me to places unfathomable, insurmountable.
Ten tone rows reassuring as stepping stones through swamps
of uncertainty. Ten fingers, ten toes, this numbered breath.
     I hold tight to numbers, my fortress,
the ring of formulae that keeps me safe.
Only Number can touch me now.

Dearest Glenn,

It was the Traditional Chinese Medicine doctor who finally named the crackling in my hearing ear. Eustachian tubes, she said. They too, were damaged. Now I am a human barometer. When the air pressure falls, when I drive up a hill, I have to yawn as if I've just taken an airplane ride.

The quieter it gets, the more I listen to your music. As if everything is there—beauty and calm and order. Mostly order. With Bach and you, all the puzzles are set out and all get resolved. Not puzzles even, but those Celtic knots that weave in and around each other forming patterns, messages if I could read them, but beautiful in themselves even if I can not, or on the days when I can not.

With thanks.

k.

Concerto in D Minor after Alessandro Marcello (*Adagio*) by J.S. Bach

The shelter of darkness, a greatcoat of sound.

> My hands and my shoulders,
> abstractions that succor and woo, lift me.

> A shadow turns to greet me. Twin.

I bend and it rises to me, the union
of finger and key, the music, already here.

Nonconformist Bach

Bach found God in counterpoint, the form of it.
Or is it, Bach found counterpoint in God?
Either. A divine architecture, extraordinary juncture.
There was constancy and immutability and constant effort.
Nothing ambiguous about their relationship.
All other questions died in static.

Bach's participation in helping bridge a wide valley is misunderstood.
One can safely say he was a salesman, out of place.
He did not deny grandeur but there was a question of style.
It was almost the age of the atom, after all.

It is tempting to give an analysis, to submit
to the fearful rites of belief and disbelief
but speaking in a general way, Bach's was a time of extraordinary
spiritual compromise. There were many voices,
a heart's rest of chorales and concerti, structural phenomena latent within.

But in an age of reason, he was essentially
unreasonable; relinquished formulae and found form.
He withdrew into an idealized world of uncompromised invention
and there he solidly encamped.
Stand firm! he told himself. And sat astride his life
finding its themes, over and over.

When Bach died, something was forever lost.

This is the case: Bach's participation in musical history
makes sense of the world.

Dear Glenn,

Last week in my dreams I climbed a high tower. A single bird—a fat black-winged thing so heavy it can't fly—perches in front of me on the wall, a mummy's bird that should have been pushed out of the nest a long time ago. The bird sits clumsily on my head, its tail blocking my left ear.

I can't hear, I tell it. Shoo! And it does but minutes later crawls pitifully up the side of the tower, a plea in its eyes.

The next night the crow comes back. He (she?) sits on the stone balustrade of my tower and this time I only watch. She's impatient, a bit cynical—a worldly crow who has something to tell me but I don't speak Crow.

She surprises me—this bird who last week only crawled, now flies off the parapet and back to me and a voice says, You knew I could. It's the crow, talking. We've connected.

And suddenly I understand that I'm furious and I let fly; I scream gusts of wind that soar from my mouth as banners of colour—red and turquoise and yellow rage pillowing in the wind as the crow dives and swoops among them. She likes it that I get mad.

Your dream, about the spaceship—about standing at the edge of the universe and looking back at all of us—the great quiet of that, makes for a more peaceful night than this!

Yours in dreaming,

k.

How It Looks: Gould at Age Fifty

I'm not beautiful any more. Almost simian—this sunken brow, sideburns,
these preternaturally long fingers, small dark hairs on the back
of hands curled like claws (Mine! Mine!) over the keyboard.
How they have hurt me! And this crumpled grey jacket with the wrinkled,
too-long arms and twisted tie, my hair unwashed and pushed askew
behind any ear (today my left), and ah, these too large listening ears
and muttering lips—all, all hopelessly now, for years, out of my control.

Whose control then? Who directs each note that graces me still water clear,
a bright light shining from the chest of the piano, my trembling hands....
Who, I say?

Who cares? The body sits, waits. And I can taste it, honey,
blood pounding, the vein that pulses in my forehead,
the begging, begging, begging of my left hand until the music comes
back, breaks over me and I breathe again.
And after, all the beauty out of me. Empty. To wait again.

Pain

No feeling.

The thing I live for
that lives through me

stoppered.

Today

my hands don't speak.
Or yesterday.

Tomorrow?

Dear Glenn,

Yesterday I came out of the Ear Nose Throat doctor's office, furious.
I've tried it all—drugs, massage, chiropractic, acupuncture. I've gone
to ear doctors, neck doctors, jaw doctors, even a podiatrist (your gait
can throw off your bone structure which can throw off...). I've had
blood tests and CT scans and an MRI that show there's no syphilis
and no tumours but they still don't know what caused this deafness
(virus?), no idea how to fix it and they say a hearing aid won't help.
What now? What do you do when none of your tools work?

I know you're scared too, about your hands, your arms, sickness,
everything. A friend told me yesterday, It's OK to be scared. Practice
compassion for yourself. How often do people say that—love yourself,
damaged as you are?

Lucky again?
k.

The Tea Cup

> *I suddenly felt that...maybe...if I look at the Goldberg*
> *Variations again, I could find a way of making some*
> *sort of almost arithmetical correspondence between*
> *the theme and the subsequent variations.*
>
> —Glenn Gould

All the curly detail of napkin and fishhook and clock. How can one
live? The infinite details of dress. Who could know what it is to
replace a button. Thread? To cook means to plan. All I can do: make
tea, drink water. The rest I can buy. Or Ray does it for me. I'm
fine. I'm fine. I don't see the details. Or nothing but. Pick any act,
one—like taking this tea cup from the kitchen to my chair. First the
epic of brewing, then the full cup on my way past an odyssey of books
and notes, edits to the next text, gulls and the sound of wind. And
the temperature across Canada—look! It continues to rise and fall
unmarked if I don't stop and write it from the television: plus six in
Vancouver, minus fifteen in Toronto, minus forty-five in Regina now,
the national low and I have to know, I feel it, in my blood pounding, the
cuff here, 146 over 112 and only moments ago it was almost normal.
How can I live? Do you see it now? The details? I'll read for rest, but
there, I'd almost forgotten the music, the score I was going to—the
Goldbergs. Again. I will think it through, the pace, relationships,
one tragic note, one burning vessel after another in Bach's process
of helping Goldberg lull his lord to sleep, to sleep and what is this
up-knocked over now, a small waterfall of tea, brassy and sweet, the
cool wet on my knees, a triage of notes under my tongue, my fingers,
song taking me now so nothing matters but this light bright shining
and I've got it now the pace, a tender drip off the coffee table lip the

exact beat of Bach's heart, the metre and measure I've been seeking for the first to the fourteenth and damn the twenty-third variation. They ask me by whose permission do I slow the traditional pace, the way it's always been done? Easy, it's easy, it's by the measure of this tea, falling now, by the certainty of my blood, by the arms that reach and swallow me in music, one variation, five and ten and on. Now how does it come to be morning? What happened to the night? My tea?

The Goldberg Variations (1981)

I hover, cuffs flapping, dive,
into an oh-so-independently-minded harmonic design.
I'm a bird let loose, black and white wings rising.

Transition.
Always a time of tension. For just a second, I don't know
where I am going.

Ah, but it was a tease! A joke! Of course I knew.
Or do now.
But there, for just a second,
the fabulous terror of not knowing, before
one begins. Again.

You ask what I see when I play?
I see trembling but not servility.
I see heaven, Bach's slow steady step,
the cameraman frozen, caught with me
for a second. Then I'm not looking anywhere
but inward, exultant, each variation its own
related voice until the end, the very last one.

Don't, the *aria da capo* says, *Don't leave me
alone here!* Pain of being torn, letting go
one finger at a time. A ring to remember me by—
small, hard, perfect—something
just a little dangerous.

Dear Glenn,

*I've found the ENT doctor I'll stick with. He summed it up, said,
Hearing in your right ear is normal but in your left you're profoundly
deaf. You're going to have to see people's faces when they speak,
you'll be reading their lips and watching the expression on their faces
because you'll be less sensitive to tone. Then he just looked at me, as
if it were my turn.*

*It's not entirely bad, I say. Suddenly I'm consoling him. It was only
after I lost my hearing that I started listening to Glenn Gould.
And Bach, I've found Bach.*

*As I left, he shook my hand. Take care, he said, and I felt he was the
one hurting.*

> *Your friend through all of it,*
> *k.*

Fragment

Fragmented, you say?
I take it all apart, howl

       one Bach two Bach...

When I broke, I examined each finger as ruby, pearl.
Why be distracted by the whole necklace—worse—the neck that bears it?

Better to turn it over as I do, then, not distracted
by the dazzle of flesh, each star shines alone, brilliant, in its place, in a line.

When stars come to earth over water,
you can enter them.

I open with logic and still my blood pressure rises, 148 over 118,
like a diamond's edge, cracking the crystal walls of reason's castle.

I can pound at the piano all I like, cold alphabet of reason,
no steam rising here. There's no sound like it. No sound.

Like me, those stars, shiny on the outside. But inside?
When I'm alone?

A coat that fits all too well, too tightly even, as I age.
A broken, burning skin.

The running average of my blood pressure, mounting.
Perhaps if I redefine "normal" I shall not be alarmed?

I was wrong about the stars. When they come to earth
they are swallowed whole by dark water.

Dis, dis = not to. Integrate. Not to
enter. Pressure. Rising.

> *...three Bach, to thee I roar.*

The Faces We Wear: Last Interview

I did agree to this interview but I prefer you tell no one.
    I've been too much alone of late and
            an earthy heaviness   has come over me.

Let me begin again.

I am planning a lecture that will begin: *Walk with me.*
Epic implied. Absolutely necessary it sounds
       unearthly   numinous   from a source
highly personal,
             sensual even.

Not my usual studio sound but just once, something
        unedited   something
                         wildly beautiful,
  its roots in the Unconscious.

It shall be an upward aria
      yearning

           toward Mother?   Or
   another power perhaps....

Not a lecture, you say? A composition then—
      yes, another sound, something like opera
   that lets me be lost.

The truth is
I can't stand Pain.

Nor am I a stranger to Fear.
            I am afraid to wake up
                         afraid of light—
      the terrifying net of it.

Don't even pretend anymore.
Take a pill.

I live a private life, hardly swank   yet
        people find anything   everything about me
              irresistible.

Witness:
yesterday someone said I am an "iconic" figure—
        another appalling variation on a life in public,
            the shackle of it.

I prefer not to look the person I'm talking to in the eye,
    drag my friends into my presence over the telephone.
I'm the reluctant piano player trying to articulate properly
      a single moment   silence

        but my music,
now that is your question—what you came for—

      the music I offer shall be utterly committed
      and the moments of silence
        integral. You'll hardly recognize
      the person who wrote it.

The original act shall be my childhood, all
crescendi and diminuendi, a life
            strange to me   looking back.

I shall call my opera *Lily* and explore the liminal
by looking directly at the music.   It will stay with you
forever   this piece, every voice
            accounted for.

Ah yes, the interview.
Pardon my confusion.
                Tea?

As introduction, I shall say I am a graduate
    of the Barnum & Bailey School. My life has been
        that strange to me.
            But I distill it here to

            Bach, Bach, Bach, Bach, Bach, Bach, Bach. Or,
                for want of a better word,
                        Bach.

It's a joke! There is no better word!

Music, like poetry, is heard in the right brain
    so I shall perform this, my last composition, to the left
        —in chanting voice—

                an entire hymnal
                without any
                God

        not even Metre

a hymnal (hummable) ineffable,
                              ever-changing.

I shall brush aside all fear—did I say that?—and people
(mere distraction)
        for a great chorus.

Not opera? All right, a symphony then!
One hundred instruments,
                              but voice-like.

  It shall be urgent. It shall be urgent

        and slow.
                    And the final line—after a moment of
                              perfectly

    articulated

      silence

                shall be:

Dearest Glenn,

Last night for the first time I saw you on TV. Saw your body gone, only holding you—frail sac—while you took us all away. Did you see—after—how we ran along behind, begging?

Love,

k.

Lists: a found(erring) poem

I make lists, numbers of numbers, the numbers on cheques, the letters covering:

Ra... No, the feeling is wrong. Again.

Ray (it's a Lucky, I think). *Ray, These go to (Mr.) Chris Nelson*

A thicket one has to plough through.
Bramble and ash.

Ray. These go to Mr. (say it again) *Chris Nelson, 51*

If I keep hold. Help me. I mean

Ray   These go

No. Walls glow. Press back. It must be for another day.

Ecstasy

Celebrating
necessitates
static mobility as opposed
to upward mobility

Celebrating reminds one of
                              (possess) i.e. ecstatic state
what one does not usually have
i.e. the exceptional state,
and to be reminded of that
is to imperil it and to make
it increasingly unlikely that one ever will possess it

Scarecrow

Knuckle bone. Knee bone.
          It's all a lightness and I am hungry for a heavier place.

What is life but an intention, interlude that if we play it well
          takes one small step toward sacred ground?
          Will there be a footprint when I am gone?

I dreamed I stood at the edge of the universe
          watching, but you could not see.
          Now the wind has found me. My empty arms
          reach, embrace the hallowed silence.

Mother, the Body Betrayed Me

I could edit my recorded performance to a single sixteenth note,
piano tuned to a delicacy. But flesh?
It creaked and staggered on regardless of doctors, hot water, massage.

I found marks on my stomach, worried, took notes,
was relieved they washed off in the bath—only ink.
But near misses. Remember the time I had the first five symptoms
of polio and phoned to warn I wouldn't show up for the concert
if the sixth appeared? Pure luck when it didn't.

Only nerves, they said. Only nerves, twisted my gut, my joints,
sent shooting pains down my arms to my fingers,
these hands, the key to my prison. Only pills—
ointments, potions, castings, bizarre and otherwise—welcomed me,
protected the means for me to escape this rattling form.

And then defeated me.

But they sent my music in a spaceship, *Voyager*,
perhaps to some larger intelligence. So look up, Mother!
To the edge of the world. It is me. And Bach,
playing the music of the spheres, every blessed note of it
just as I dreamed.

In the cold, under clear stars, you will hear us.
And now good night, Mother, good night.

Epilogue

Dear Glenn,

I planned for one whole year and when the plan fell through, planned again to see you, or what you left. When the archivist's email asked what I wanted to see, "Which of his realia?" I'd never heard the word, idly checked the list, ticking here and there. A coat? Sure. Eyeglasses? Sounded good. A book, an amulet, a chair? It wasn't until Gatineau, when the archivist's helper led me down a sterile beige corridor past the thin grey outlines of windowless doors and stopped in front of one, nondescript as the rest, pushed it open and gestured for me to step inside—it wasn't until then that I knew what I had done. Even then.

We stepped into a vault like my old university library, a vast metal tank six storeys high, sealed for control of temperature, moisture, air, with shelves rising through it—storey after storey of perforated metal to let the air pass, let nothing mould or dry, only a metal grill to walk upon with sheets of plywood laid for the timid who might not be pleased to look past their feet at the shelves below. I step through the grey door into the world of realia. On the shelves—this is not a library—small treasures culled from the lives and closets of those once among us. Here are the hooked rugs of Emily Carr, pysanky—hand painted Ukrainian eggs, Iroquois lacrosse sticks (Haudenosaunee, the young woman says, when I ask the Iroquois name), Pierre Elliot Trudeau's hat, the passport of a 1930s Italian immigrant—all bric-a-brac of the ones who carved out what it means to be Canadian. Realia. I follow the young woman down a long echoing row through perfectly preserved air, trying not to imagine the floor as it shakes beneath me, to where two large tables are spread with a thin cloth of white foam so nothing can slip. Laid out precisely on the top, as if on exhibit, are a navy blue winter coat, heavy brown eyeglasses, a book—all the items on my casual list—and beside them, a coffee table and armchair.

Here is your coat. Your eyeglasses. Your coffee table and chair. Not the piano chair—that, no one is allowed to touch. That, I've already seen, behind glass. But here your living room armchair—ratty old yellow thing—and to one side, a pair of white cotton gloves. Something sucks the air out of my chest. The archivist's helper nods. I don the gloves. She sits in a straight-backed chair in an aisle a few feet away, and watches.

I take a deep breath. Lay one hand upon your shoe. Do you laugh? Have I ever been this close before? Foolish woman, you are thinking. And I don't care. Another breath. Surrender to being a groupie, another fan possessed by you, rub one finger over the polished toe of your brown Oxford. Was it you who polished it last? Or Ray, your trusty "man"? Twenty-three years since you left them. I look over my left shoulder.

The woman watches. I raise my eyebrow and she nods. I lift your shoe, put it to my nose and inhale. Again. Faint whiff of leather. I almost laugh as I put it down again. Foolish woman indeed! Then a trinket of yours that I handle with more reverence than I would touch a saint's bones. Silly. I surrender.

Your eyeglasses now—large, round, brown. I've seen them on your face, the films. I lift them, carefully, slip them on. Now I am looking at the world through your eyes, Glenn. I see.

I have circled your coat but now I approach it. This navy blue wool you wore no matter what the weather, with this scarf and these gloves and this hat. I lay both my hands on the coat as if to hold it from rising, notice the missing button, the long white hairs of a dog on the front. You loved dogs to the end. I wonder how it fit you, this coat? Glance over and the woman is on her cellphone, facing away, bent forward as if to muffle her conversation. She would never agree to this. It would be so simple, only a moment to lift your coat from the table and slip it on, to stand inside, with you, my arms too short, my body lost inside its blue bulk. It wouldn't take long and this would be you: long arms, thick middle, not-so-very-long legs. I breathe, so close, the young woman still on her phone. The coat lifts, a new life, even so brief, and subsides slowly as if getting used to being empty again.

But the woman rises now. Time to go, Glenn. When the grey door closes crisply behind me with a breath of purified air, I am satisfied. We've had a good visit, you and I. As if inside the warm blue serge of your greatcoat, we are met, at last.

Biographical Note

The incidents in this book, though clearly filtered through my perceptions of Glenn Gould, and with a touch of poetic licence, are based on fact.

Glenn Gould (1932-1982) was born and raised and lived all his life in Toronto, Ontario, Canada. His mother, Florence, and father, Herbert, were both musical and Florence was determined her only child would be musical as well. At the age of three it was discovered Glenn had perfect pitch and formal lessons, with his mother as teacher, began when he was four. Florence taught Glenn to hum, to hear the music in his mind before his fingers played it. It was a habit he never broke and years later, in concerts and when recording, he drove some audience members and his sound engineers wild with his singing.

Gould was very close to his mother. At about age twelve he told Robert Fulford—one of his only childhood friends—that at the Gould summer cottage he and his father alternated nights of sleeping with her.

Gould's second and only other piano teacher (from the age of ten) was Alberto Guerrero, a Chilean, whose influence Gould later oddly denied. Guerrero taught Gould, among other techniques, to sit low and close to the keyboard, reaching up to the keys from below. It was from Guerrero that Gould learned his love of Bach and Schoenberg.

Gould always adored animals and owned a succession of dogs as well as other creatures, including a fully functioning skunk. He claimed as one of his "greatest achievements" persuading his father, an avid fisherman, to give up fishing.

Gould's passion was Bach and the architecture—the "question and answer" structure—of counterpoint. But his tastes were eclectic: he also loved Wagner, the music of the twelve-tone composers including

Schoenberg and Webern (who showed, he said "a pure contrapuntal craftsmanship" not seen since Bach), the arch-Romantic music of Richard Strauss and the pop sounds of Barbra Streisand and Petula Clark.

From 1950 on, Gould performed extensively on radio and later television for the Canadian Broadcasting Corporation (CBC), but his international debut as a pianist was on January 2, 1955 in Washington, D.C. and on January 11 in New York City. In the small NY audience was David Oppenheim, director of artists for Columbia Masterworks, who the following morning offered Gould a contract, "The first time they have ever signed an artist just on the strength of his debut," as Gould's manager, Walter Homberger, liked to boast. It was the first time Columbia signed a Canadian and Gould would stay with Columbia (now SONY BMG Masterworks) for the rest of his career.

For his first recording, Gould chose the then-rarely played Goldberg Variations by J.S. Bach. It became an overnight sensation and has been continuously in print ever since. In 1981, shortly before his early death by stroke, the Goldbergs were one of the few pieces he re-recorded.

Glenn Gould read voraciously. Two of his favourite novels were William Santayana's *The Last Puritan* and Natsume Sōseki's *The Three-Cornered World* (see Notes).

It disturbed Gould that people thought him "eccentric." One of the many reasons for such a judgement was his use of the chair his father built him to use as a piano bench. It was a folding chair with screws soldered to each leg so Gould could adjust it for the height and angles he preferred. He carried it with him everywhere as it slowly disintegrated under him (partly from fans and musicians stealing bits) until it was a mere wooden skeleton, but he used it exclusively—creaks and all—when he played, until his death.

He had other habits that were considered eccentric, for example, he wore baggy clothes and stocking feet or untied his shoes on stage. He placed glasses of water on the piano, thumped his feet, hummed, and conducted himself as he played. He wore gloves, layers of warm clothing and a hat regardless of the temperature, shunned daylight and worked only at night (his favourite colours were midnight blue and battleship grey). He often chose unusual interpretations of music, including slow tempos. He avoided personal touch, instead preferring to speak to friends—endlessly—on the telephone, at night. "Friends," he said toward the end of his life, "are about as important to me as food. As I grow older I find more and more that I can do without them."

He was physically clumsy and, as his friend John Roberts reports, "often seemed incapable of carrying a cup of coffee from one room to another without spilling it." He was also superstitious, believing in lucky and unlucky numbers and dates. Robert Fulford insists that Gould was "not a kook, not eccentric. He was a great artist in great emotional difficulty for much of his life." Some have suggested that some of Gould's "eccentricities" and other traits such as his extraordinary musical memory, were signs of Asperger's Syndrome, a high-functioning form of autism. If so, they are a confirmation that disability from one perspective, is brilliance from another.

Gould hated live audiences, perhaps a part of his passionate dislike of any kind of competition. (Before a Bach concert at Canada's Stratford Music Festival, he explained to the audience that he found automatic applause after a performance, "an easily induced mob reaction" and requested they not applaud. He emphasized it by having the lights dimmed to black. The audience was confused.) It is one reason why Gould far preferred the splendid isolation—and technical control—of the recording studio, and in 1964 at the age of thirty-one, he stopped all public performance and instead, recorded exclusively in NY for Sony Columbia and in Toronto for CBC radio and television.

Gould's curiosity, enthusiasm and intelligence took him wherever there was sound. He didn't cook for himself and one day, sitting in a local restaurant, he noticed that the rise and fall of conversation at the tables around him followed a musical, contrapuntal pattern. This led to some extraordinary experiments in radio. John Roberts at the CBC gave Gould a small office and a brilliant technician, Lorne Tulk. With Tulk and others, Gould created a series of radio documentaries called *The Solitude Trilogy* of which the first, *The Idea of North* was commissioned by CBC for 1967, Canada's 100th birthday.

Though he loved driving—with heat and radio turned on high—Gould's friends and colleagues report that he was a terrible driver. The Canadian north fascinated him and he loved to drive his black Lincoln Continental (dubbed "Longfellow") north to Wawa, Ontario, on the shore of Lake Superior, rent a motel and work on music or radio pieces. However, because of his fear of flying, a train trip to Churchill was as far north as he ever ventured.

Most people knew Glenn Gould as unfailingly polite and respectful though he was always clear—and forceful—on how he thought any piece of music should be interpreted. He loved puzzles and jokes and could drive people mad with his games of "Twenty Questions."

From early childhood, Gould was a hypochondriac and in the mid-1970s he went through a period of being particularly concerned about the failure of his hands to produce music for him at his command. He continued to produce brilliant recordings (especially once his favourite site, the Eaton Auditorium, was returned to him) but his notebooks suggest increasingly desperate attempts to try and keep order in a world that seemed to be dissolving for him. He kept endless lists (with mathematical relationships of the lists), of the weather across Canada, of his blood pressure, stock market figures, and of people's names. No one knows how, or if, the many pills and drugs he was taking at the time might have accelerated this, but his biographer, Kevin Bazzana, reports that in the nine months before Gould died, between January and September 1982, Glenn Gould was prescribed (by various doctors who didn't know about each other) more than two thousand pills, many of them serious drugs including Valium, Aldomet and Librax. It couldn't have helped that, although he was a teetotaler, he had terrible eating habits and ate only once a day: scrambled eggs, tea and salad.

When Gould died of a massive stroke a few days after his fiftieth birthday, one half of his estate went to the Toronto Humane Society and the other half to the Salvation Army.

Glenn Gould is acknowledged as one of the world's finest interpreters of J.S. Bach. In 1977 when the US launched the *Voyager* spacecraft, one of the "messages" on it was a copy of Gould playing the Prelude and Fugue in C major from Book 2 of Bach's *The Well-Tempered Clavier*. One day it will, perhaps, show another life form what we here on earth consider most beautiful in our civilization.

Notes:

Page 22. *My Plans for the School Year* by Glenn Gould, Grade 13. A school essay in Gould's handwriting, Library and Archives Canada, Glenn Gould fonds (MUS 109/23, 127, 3-4).

Page 52. *The Last Puritan: A Memoir in the Form of a Novel*, was the only novel written by philosopher, George Santayana (1863-1952). The book, about a man who struggles to deal with his own puritan-ism, was one of Gould's favourites.

Page 58. *Burlesca* is an Italian word meaning "a musical joke." The answer to the riddle is a piano.

Page 64. *The Idea of North* was prepared for Canada's 1967 centennial and was the first of three radio documentaries (together titled, *Solitude Trilogy*, around the theme of isolation) prepared and produced by Gould for CBC radio. In them, he used a revolutionary technique of overlapping voices he called, "contrapuntal radio." He said of the *Trilogy* that they were "as close to an autobiographical statement as I intend to get in radio."

Page 74. *The Three-Cornered World*. This novel, (Japanese title, *Kusamakura*), was written in 1906 by Japanese writer, Natsume Sōseki (1867-1916), and was one of Glenn's favourite books. He adapted it for CBC radio. Sōseki wrote, "An artist is a person who lives in the triangle which remains after the angle which we may call common sense has been removed from this four-cornered world."

Page 79. *The Golden Number* (also known as the Golden Mean or Golden Ratio) is a ratio of 1.618 which, since the Greeks, has been thought to create the most aesthetically pleasing proportions in all structures. This ratio is considered a mathematical constant and has many fascinating properties, including in its applications to the human body (as in Michelangelo's drawing of the Vitruvian Man). The Golden Number is related to what is called symbolic or sacred mathematics, which aims to understand nature in mathematical or geometrical terms.

How do you plant ten flowers in five rows and still have four flowers in each?

Page 85. *Nonconformist Bach.* This poem is the fruit of a writing exercise in which I took dozens of words and phrases from three sources, jumbled them and put them back together as a poem. The sources are: Annie Finch, "Walk with Me: On Poetry and Music," in *The Body of Poetry: Essays on Women, Form, and the Poetic Self* (2005); "Glenn Gould, Art of the Fugue," in *The Glenn Gould Reader*, Ed. Tim Page; and an advertising flyer for men's clothing.

Page 101. *Lists.* Sections in italics were notes made by Gould on long sheets of yellow foolscap, referred to as his "notepads" by biographers. Library and Archives Canada, Glenn Gould fonds (MUS 109/16.50, 56-59).

Page 102. *Ecstasy.* From Glenn Gould notepads. Library and Archives, Canada. Glenn Gould fonds (MUS 109/23,93, 1).

Page 120. "I think that if I were required to spend the rest of my life..." Glenn Gould in a letter dated May 22, 1967 to Miss Debbie Barker, a fan in Delhi, Ontario, Canada. From Roberts and Guertin, Eds. *Glenn Gould: Selected Letters*, p. 102.

Selected Sources:

The following were among the most helpful books and films among the many I read and watched to help me understand the life and work of Glenn Gould. I haven't listed the music I listened to; if you're interested in Gould, I simply recommend you start listening to him play Bach, and spread out from there.

Books:

Bazzana, Kevin. *Wondrous Strange: The Life and Art of Glenn Gould* (2003).

Carroll, Jock. *Glenn Gould: Some Portraits of the Artist as a Young Man* (1995).

Friedrich, Otto. *Glenn Gould: A Life and Variations* (1989).

Glenn Gould: A Life in Pictures. Foreword by Yo-Yo Ma, Introduction by Tim Page (2002).

Grandin, Temple. *Thinking in Pictures: and Other Reports from My Life with Autism* (1995).

Hafner, Katie. *A Romance on Three Legs: Glenn Gould's Obsessive Quest for the Perfect Piano* (2008).

Kazdin, Andrew. *Glenn Gould at Work: Creative Lying* (1989).

John McGreevy, ed. (and the author of introduction) *Glenn Gould by Himself and His Friends* (1983).

Ostwald, Peter F. *Glenn Gould: The Ecstasy and Tragedy of Genius* (1997).

Page, Tim, ed. *The Glenn Gould Reader* (1990). First published 1984.

Payzant, Geoffrey. *Glenn Gould: Music and Mind* (2005). First published 1984.

Roberts, John P.L., ed. *The Art of Glenn Gould: Reflections of a Musical Genius* (1999).

____. and Ghyslaine Guertin, Eds. *Glenn Gould: Selected Letters* (1992).

Schneider, Michael S. *A Beginner's Guide to Constructing the Universe: The Mathematical Archetypes of Nature, Art, and Science. A Voyage from 1 to 10* (1995).

Radio:

Gould, Glenn. *Solitude Trilogy: Three Sound Documentaries.* (*The Idea of North* {1967}, *The Latecomers* {1969}, *The Quiet in the Land* {1977}. Prepared and produced by Glenn Gould for the Canadian Broadcasting Corporation (1992).

Films:

Glenn Gould: The Alchemist. A film by Bruno Monsaingeon, directed by François-Louis Ribadeau. EMI Classics. Ideale Audience International (2002).

____. *Extasis.* CBC Home Video and Kultur (1993).

____.*The Goldberg Variations* from *Glenn Gould Plays Bach.* A film by Bruno Monsaingeon. Sony Classical (2000).

____. *Hereafter.* A film by Bruno Monsaingeon, Ideale Audience International (2005, 2006).

____. *Life and Times.* CBC Home Video and Kultur (1998).

____.*The Russian Journey.* CBC Home Video and Kultur (2002).

Acknowledgements

The poem "Sleepless" is dedicated to Lorne Tulk.

"The Tea Cup" is for Brian Tate.

"The Goldberg Variations (1981) that begins, "I hover..." is for David Carlin.

"Fragment" is for Jay MillAr.

Many people have helped me, non-musician, to understand Gould and the music he loved, particularly Bach. I am especially grateful to Gould's Canadian biographer, Kevin Bazzana, who generously kept me on track with details of music and biography. Any errors, of course, are stubbornly my own.

Other vital musical aid came from Brian Tate who shared his love of Bach over and over. Thanks also to Andrew Clarke for help with the math, to Joy Coghill-Thorne for connections, and to Elke Stoll for health and to my family for cheering.

I am grateful to Lorne Tulk who spent a day showing me Gould's old hangouts and talking about his years as Gould's CBC technician, and to Verne Edquist, Mario Prizek and Tom Shipton who also graciously spoke about their time with Gould. Thanks to the archivists at CBC, at Library and Archives Canada and at the Museum of Civilization, especially Gail Donald, Barbara Clarke, Maureen Nevins, Brenda Muir, Carmelle Bégin and Constance Nebel. Thanks to SONY BMG especially Tom Tierney and Che Williams. A special thanks to Don Hunstein for photos and to Faye Perkins for using her many hats to facilitate all things Gouldian.

This manuscript has been vastly improved by the careful poetic eye of Sandy Shreve, Betsy Warland and George McWhirter. Special thanks for Betsy's question and for tutoring me through the white space. Thanks also for the insight and encouragement given in various forms by other poets along the way, including Tana Runyon, Carla Hartsfield, Jay MillAr, Barry Dempster and John Thompson, for *Stilt Jack*.

Thanks to Malaspina-University College (now Vancouver Island University) for financial support during the research for this book.

Some of these poems have previously appeared in the following publications: the *Literary Review of Canada*, *Glenn Gould: A Musical Force*, *RHYTHM Poetry Magazine* and *In Fine Form: The Canadian Book of Form Poetry*.

I thank Vici Johnstone for taking on the publication of this book, and thanks always to John Steeves who doesn't just endure but supports the process and the processor, no matter how three-cornered she gets. And of course, Glenn. We have had a rough but exciting friendship.

Permissions:

"My Plans for the School Year," material in the poems "Lists" and "Ecstasy," and the Gould letter that forms the epitaph ("I think if I were required...") quoted with permission from the Glenn Gould Estate. All photos with permission of SONY BMG (Don Hunstein, photographer).

The epigraph to "Shucking Genius" is with permission from the poet.

The line "the crystal walls of reason's castle" in "Fragment" is by Paul Youngquist, "Madness and Blake's Myth," in Daniel Deardorff's, *The Other Within* cited with permission of Penn State Press.

I think that if I were required to spend the rest of my life
on a desert island, and to listen or play the music of any one
composer during all that time, that composer would almost
certainly be Bach. I really can't think of any other music
which is so all-encompassing, which moves me so deeply
and so consistently, and which, to use a rather imprecise word,
is valuable beyond all of its skill and brilliance for something
more meaningful than that—its humanity.

—Glenn Gould